What We Do in Fall

by JoAnn Early Macken

LOOK!
BOOKS™

Red Chair Press   Egremont, Massachusetts

Look! Books are produced and published by Red Chair Press:

Red Chair Press LLC   PO Box 333   South Egremont, MA 01258-0333

www.redchairpress.com

 FREE activity page from www.redchairpress.com/free-activities

Publisher's Cataloging-In-Publication Data

Names: Macken, JoAnn Early, 1953-

Title: What we do in fall / by JoAnn Early Macken.

Description: Egremont, Massachusetts : Red Chair Press, [2018] | Series: Look! books : Seasons can be fun | Interest age level: 004-007. | Includes Now You Know fact-boxes, a glossary, and resources for additional reading. | Includes index. | Summary: "Making personal connections to seasonal activity is a powerful way for young readers to learn how each season differs from the others… Have you seen geese flying high? Maybe you like counting pumpkins in a field. Let's discover all the fun things to do in Fall."--Provided by publisher.

Identifiers: ISBN 978-1-63440-308-5 (library hardcover) | ISBN 978-1-63440-360-3 (paperback) | ISBN 978-1-63440-312-2 (ebook)

Subjects: LCSH: Autumn--Juvenile literature. | Amusements--Juvenile literature. | CYAC: Autumn. | Amusements.

Classification: LCC QB637.4 .M33 2018 (print) | LCC QB637.4 (ebook) | DDC 508.2 [E]--dc23

LCCN 2017947554

Photo credits: iStock except for the following; p. 3, 12, 23, 24: Shutterstock; p. 15: © Wavebreak Media ltd/Alamy; p. 21: © Media Bakery; p. 22: Anneli Höglind Thompson

Printed in the United States of America

0718 1P CGF18

Table of Contents

Autumn or Fall

In autumn, green leaves change color. They fall from the trees. Do you think this is why some people call the season Fall? Autumn or Fall, it's your call!

Hike in the Woods

Fall is a cool season. We wear warm clothes to walk in the woods. Squirrels run from tree to tree, hiding acorns. Fallen leaves cover the ground. *Crunch!*

Farmers' Market

At the farmers' market, we find corn on the cob. Flowers stand in **buckets**. Honey jars are lined up in rows. People buy apples and kale.

Back to School in September

In the morning, we wait at the corner. A yellow school bus picks us up. We ride to school with our classmates.

Class Trip

Our class visits a pumpkin farm. Horses pull us in a wagon. We ride to a **field** of orange pumpkins. They grow on long green vines. Some are big and some are small.

Leafy Fun

At home, we rake leaves into a big pile. We take turns jumping in. Leaves fly all over. We rake them all up and jump in again.

October in the Orchard

We stop at an **orchard**.
Apple and pear trees
grow in rows. People
climb ladders to pick
them. We drink apple
cider. We taste
fresh fruit.

Geese Migrate

We hear geese honk.
We look up in the sky.
In Fall, geese fly to
warmer places. The **flock**
looks like an arrow
pointing south. *Good
idea geese!*

November Feast

Friends and family join us for Thanksgiving. We share a special meal. We are glad to be together.

Good to Know

Thanksgiving in Canada is a holiday in October. In the United States it is in November. Both holidays celebrate the fall harvest.

Words to Keep

bucket: a pail

field: an area of open land with no trees or buildings

flock: a group of animals such as birds

migrate: to move from one place to another, usually at regular times of the year

orchard: a place where fruit or nut trees grow

Learn More at the Library

Books (Check out these books to learn more.)

Latta, Sara L. *Why Is It Fall?* Enslow Publishing, 2012.

Murray, Julie. *Fall.* Abdo Kids, 2016.

Schuh, Mari. *I See Fall Leaves.* Lerner Publications, 2017.

Web Sites (Ask an adult to show you these web sites.)

Easy Science for Kids
http://easyscienceforkids.com/all-about-seasons/

University of Illinois: Tree House Weather Kids
https://extension.illinois.edu/treehouse/seasons.cfm?Slide=1

Index

About the Author

JoAnn Early Macken has written more than 130 books for young children. She likes eating pumpkin pie on Thanksgiving at home in Wisconsin.